Poem Stew

Poem Stew

Poems Selected by William Cole

Pictures by Karen Ann Weinhaus

■ HarperTrophy

A Division of HarperCollinsPublishers

Library of Congress Catalog Card Number: 81-47106

ISBN 0-397-31963-0

ISBN 0-397-31964-9 (lib. bdg.)

ISBN 0-06-440136-7 (pbk.)

First Harper Trophy edition, 1983.

Grateful acknowledgment is made to the following for permission to use the material
owned by them. Every reasonable effort has been made to clear the use of the poems in
this volume with the copyright owners.

The Estates of Franklin P. Adams and Esther Root Adams for "The Groaning Board" from
Innocent Merriment by Franklin P. Adams.

Angus & Robertson Publishers for "Arbuckle Jones" from *The Ombley Gombley* by Peter
Wesley-Smith reprinted by permission of Angus & Robertson Publishers.

Richard Armour for "A Man for All Seasonings" from *The Spouse in the House* by Richard
Armour. Copyright © 1975 by Richard Armour.

Atheneum Publishers for "An Alarming Sandwich" from *One Winter Night in August and
Other Nonsense Jingles* by X. J. Kennedy (A Margaret K. McElderry Book), Copyright ©
1975 by X. J. Kennedy; for "Lasagna" from *The Phantom Ice Cream Man: More Nonsense
Verse* by X. J. Kennedy (A Margaret K. McElderry Book), Copyright © 1979 by X. J.
Kennedy; and for "O Sliver of Liver" from *O Sliver of Liver and Other Poems* by Myra
Cohn Livingston (A Margaret K. McElderry Book), Copyright © 1979 by Myra Cohn
Livingston. Used by permission of Atheneum Publishers.

Curtis Brown Agency for "Accidentally" from *No One Writes a Letter to a Snail* by Maxine
W. Kumin. Copyright © 1962 by Maxine W. Kumin. Reprinted by permission of Curtis
Brown Agency.

Contents

This book is kind of a   poem stew,
About the foods poets write   poems to;
New ones and funny old   poems too;
It shows us the many things   poems do.
I hope that they seem like good poems t'you.

Poem Stew

A Thousand Hairy Savages

A thousand hairy savages
Sitting down to lunch
Gobble gobble glup glup
Munch munch munch.

SPIKE MILLIGAN

Song of the Pop-Bottlers

Pop bottles pop-bottles
    In pop shops;
The pop-bottles Pop bottles
    Poor Pop drops.

When Pop drops pop-bottles,
    Pop-bottles plop!
Pop-bottle-tops topple!
    Pop mops slop!

Stop! Pop'll drop bottle!
    Stop, Pop, stop!
When Pop bottles pop-bottles,
    Pop-bottles pop!

MORRIS BISHOP

Tableau at Twilight

I sit in the dusk. I am all alone.
Enter a child and an ice-cream cone.

A parent is easily beguiled
By sight of this coniferous child.

The friendly embers warmer gleam,
The cone begins to drip ice cream.

Cones are composed of many a vitamin.
My lap is not the place to bitamin.

Although my raiment is not chinchilla,
I flinch to see it become vanilla.

Coniferous child, when vanilla melts
I'd rather it melted somewhere else.

Exit child with remains of cone.
I sit in the dusk. I am all alone,

Muttering spells like an angry Druid,
Alone, in the dusk, with the cleaning fluid.

OGDEN NASH

Aunt Nerissa's Muffin

It was touching when I started
    For to run away to sea.
All the town was brokenhearted,
    As I knowed that they would be.

And me Aunt Nerissa Duffin,
    Standing weeping on the spot,
Handed me a graham muffin
    And she says, "Take care, it's hot!

"Though you've been a bit unruly
    We are awful fond of ye.
I remain yours very truly,
    Ever thine, Nerissa D."

Then she had a bad hy-sterick
    And she fell down in a faint
Till they raised her with a derrick—
    Light and airy?—Aunty ain't.

So I left Nerissa Duffin
    Waving of her handkerchee
And I took her graham muffin
    As I sadly put to sea.

Says the mate, "Why don't ye eat it?"
    But me youthful head I shook;
For I knowed—nor dare repeat it—
    Aunt Nerissa couldn't cook.

Then we sailed to De Janeiro
    Where we spent a week in Wales,
And enjoyed ourselves in Cairo
    Tossing oysters to the whales.

Next we visited Virginia
    Loading almanacks as freight,
Then we tarried in Sardinia
    Where we caught sardines for bait.

But when it was late September
    Something frightened of us all;
What it was I don't remember,
    Why it was I don't recall.

But I says to Capting Casmar,
    "Be we on the land or sea?"
But the Capting had the asthma
    And he wouldn't speak to me.

Then the pilot on the trestle
    He began to rip and snort
And he hollered, "Back the vessel!"
    Till the ship arrived in port.

And there stood Nerissa Duffin
    Waiting for me on the spot
And she says, "Where is me muffin?
    Wretched boy, have you fergot?"

"Do you think I could ferget it?"
    Answers I in grief and pain,
"Saved!" she cried. "I thought you'd et it"—
    And she swooned away again.

WALLACE IRWIN

The Man in the Onion Bed

I met a man in an onion bed.
He was crying so hard his eyes were red.
And the tears ran off the end of his nose
As he ate his way down the onion rows.

He ate and he cried, but for all his tears
He sang: "Sweet onions, oh my dears!
I love you, I do, and you love me,
But you make me as sad as a man can be."

JOHN CIARDI

9

My Wise Old Grandpapa

When I was but a little chap
My grandpapa said to me,
'You'll need to know your manners, son
When you go out to tea.

'Remove the shells from hard-boiled eggs,
Make sure your hat's on straight,
Pour lots of honey on your peas
To keep them on the plate.

'Blow daintily upon your tea
To cool it to your taste,
And always pick bones thoroughly,
With due regard for waste.

'Be heedful of your partners' needs,
Attend their every wish;
When passing jelly, cream or jam,
Make sure they're in the dish.

'When eating figs or coconuts,
To show you are refined,
Genteely gnaw the centres out
And throw away the rind.

'If you should accidentally gulp
Some coffee while it's hot,
Just raise the lid politely and
Replace it in the pot.

'Don't butter ice cream when it's warm,
Or drink soup through a straw.'
Thus spoke my wise old grandpapa
When I was only four.

WILBUR G. HOWCROFT

On Eating Porridge Made of Peas

Peas porridge hot,
Peas porridge—hold!
Who eats peas porridge?
Who is so bold?

I know I never munch
Peas porridge for my lunch,
&, as for dinner,
Peas porridge is no winner.

Peas porridge ice cold,
Peas porridge tepid,
Who eats peas porridge?
Who could be so stupid?

Peas porridge nine days old—ugh!
I think I'd prefer to eat a rug.

LOUIS PHILLIPS

Rhinoceros Stew

If you want to make a rhinoceros stew
all in the world that you have to do
is skin a rhinoceros
                cut it in two
and stew it and stew it and stew it.

When it's stewed so long that you've quite forgot
what it is that's bubbling in the pot
dish it up promptly
                serve it hot
and chew it and chew it and chew it
AND CHEW IT AND CHEW IT AND CHEW IT
and chew it and chew it and chew it
and chew it and chew it and chew it
and—

MILDRED LUTON

13

A Generous Man

What I like
(And I will share)
Is the simplest
Kind of fare.
Like eggs of quail
And legs of frog,
From the barnyard
And the bog.
Lobster tails
And lobster claw
Are foods on which
I love to gnaw.
And I can make
Fantastic use
Of the liver
Of the goose.
A simple kind
Of food appeals,
Like caviar
And jellied eels.
With a glass
Of fine champagne,
Then another—
Then a-*gain!*
Filet mignon
(The best of steak)
What a dinner
That can make!
Among all firsts

There's nothing firster
Than stew that's made
From cream and oyster.
Allow me once
Again to say
That I will share
(If *you* will pay).

WILLIAM COLE

Prunes

The prune is creased
From head to toe,
Or (if I might quote
President Taft)
"The prune is wrinkled
Fore and aft. . . ."

Pity the prune,
That misunderstood fruit.
A prune is a plum
In an unpressed suit.

LOUIS PHILLIPS

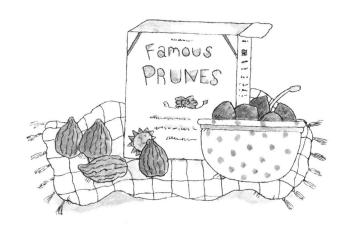

Herbert Glerbett

Herbert Glerbett, rather round,
swallowed sherbet by the pound,
fifty pounds of lemon sherbet
went inside of Herbert Glerbett.

With that glop inside his lap
Herbert Glerbett took a nap,
and as he slept, the boy dissolved,
and from the mess a thing evolved—

a thing that is a ghastly green,
a thing the world had never seen,
a puddle thing, a gooey pile
of something strange that does not smile.

Now if you're wise, and if you're sly,
you'll swiftly pass this creature by,
it is no longer Herbert Glerbett.
Whatever it is, do not disturb it.

JACK PRELUTSKY

17

Skip-Scoop-Anellie

On the island of Skip-scoop-anellie
There is made every known kind of jelly;
Kumquat and pineapple, citron and quince.
Pomegranate, apricot, all are made since
Someone discovered that jellyfish ate
Fruit from a fishhook as though it were bait.
Any particular jelly you wish,
Lower the fruit to the jellyfied fish,
After you've given it time to digest
Pull up the jellyfish. You know the rest.

TOM PRIDEAUX

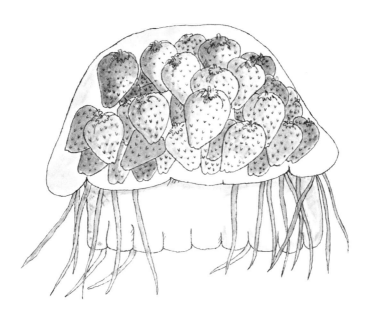

Arbuckle Jones

Arbuckle Jones
When flustered
Eats custard
With mustard.

I'm disgustard.

PETER WESLEY-SMITH

The Silver Fish

While fishing in the blue lagoon,
I caught a lovely silver fish,
And he spoke to me, "My boy," quoth he,
"Please set me free and I'll grant your wish;
A kingdom of wisdom? A palace of gold?
Or all the fancies your mind can hold?"
And I said, "O.K.," and I set him free,
But he laughed at me as he swam away,
And left me whispering my wish
Into a silent sea.

Today I caught that fish again
(That lovely silver prince of fishes),
And once again he offered me,
If I would only set him free,
Any one of a number of wishes,
If I would throw him back to the fishes.

He was delicious!

SHEL SILVERSTEIN

When Father Carves the Duck

We all look on with anxious eyes
    When father carves the duck,
And mother almost always sighs
    When father carves the duck;
Then all of us prepare to rise,
And hold our bibs before our eyes,
And be prepared for some surprise,
    When father carves the duck.

He braces up and grabs a fork
    Whene'er he carves a duck,
And won't allow a soul to talk
    Until he's carved the duck,
The fork is jabbed into the sides,
Across the breast the knife he slides,
While every careful person hides
    From flying chips of duck.

The platter's always sure to slip
    When father carves a duck,
And how it makes the dishes skip!
    Potatoes fly amuck!
The squash and cabbage leap in space,
We get some gravy in our face,
And father mutters Hindoo grace
    Whene'er he carves a duck.

We then have learned to walk around
    The dining room and pluck
From off the window sills and walls
    Our share of father's duck.
While father growls and blows and jaws
And swears the knife was full of flaws,
And mother laughs at him because
    He couldn't carve a duck.

E. V. WRIGHT

Here lies a greedy girl, Jane Bevan,
Whose breakfasts hardly ever stopped.
One morning at half past eleven
She snapped and crackled and then popped.

ANONYMOUS

When you tip the ketchup bottle,
First will come a little, then a lot'll.

ANONYMOUS

Sneaky Bill

I'm Sneaky Bill, I'm terrible mean and vicious,
I steal all the cashews
   from the mixed-nuts dishes;
I eat all the icing but I won't touch the cake,
And what you won't give me,
   I'll go ahead and take.
I gobble up the cherries from everyone's drinks,
And whenever there are sausages
   I grab a dozen links;
I take both drumsticks if
   there's turkey or chicken,
And the biggest strawberries
   are what I'm pickin';
I make sure I get the finest chop on the plate,
   And I'll eat the portions of anyone who's late!

I'm always on the spot before the dinner bell—
I guess I'm pretty awful,
             but
             I
                 do
                    eat
                     well!

WILLIAM COLE

Potato Chips

A potato chip is something
Never ceasing to amuse.
I love its funny wrinkles
And the crunchy way it chews.

ANTHONY E. GALLAGHER

There Was an Old Lady

There was an old lady
    Whose kitchen was bare,
So she woke up the cat
    Saying, "Time for some air!"

She sent him to buy her
    A can of sardines.
But the cat ambled back
    With a bagful of beans.

She sent him to buy her
    A packet of cheese.
But the cat reappeared
    With a carton of bees.

She sent him to buy her
    A brisket of beef.
But the cat hurried home
    With an Indian chief.

She sent him to buy her
    A dish of ice cream.
But the cat skated in
    With a whole hockey team.

She sent him to buy her
    A plate of spaghetti.
But the cat strutted up
    With a bride and confetti.

She sent him to buy her
    A thermos of tea.
But the cat waddled back
    With a dinosaur's knee.

The fridge was soon bulging,
    And so was the shelf.
So she phoned for a hot dog
    And fetched it herself.

DENNIS LEE

Father Loses Weight

My father lost a pound last night.
He lost it where it bounces.
He cried, "Good grief! Some gross sneak-thief
Swiped my favorite sixteen ounces!"

He turned the whole house upside-down,
Searched attic, roof, and basement.
He made us all line up and strip.
Our cat blinked in amazement.

He stomped on the bathroom scale and screamed
(He's not the best of losers)
Until the county sheriff beamed
This call to all police cruisers:

"Now hear this! Lost—one pound of weight!
All cars be on the lookout!
Last seen on Mister George McQueen
At the Cub Scout Pop corn-cookout!

"If found, the hound who pinched the pound
May be armed. This means danger!
Take care. Prepare to shoot on sight
The least suspicious stranger."

Alas, poor Dad! He felt so sad
He ate, to ease his troubles,
Six sirloin steaks, eight wedding cakes,
And ten cheeseburgers (doubles),

But all the while he gulped French fries
Adrip with salty suet
His missing pound was homeward bound
With more pounds sticking to it.

X. J. KENNEDY

Speak Clearly

You're old enough to know, my son,
    It's really awfully rude
If someone speaks when both his cheeks
    Are jammed and crammed with food.

Your mother asked you how you liked
    The onions in the stew.
You stuffed your mouth with raisin bread
    And mumbled, "Vewee goo."

Then when she asked you what you said,
    You took a drink of milk,
And all that we could understand
    Was, "Uggle gluggle skwilk."

And now you're asking me if you
    Can have more lemon jello.
Please listen carefully. "Yes, ifoo
    Arstilla ungwy fello."

MARTIN GARDNER

Mary had a little lamb,
You've heard this tale before;
But did you know
She passed her plate
And had a little more?

FOLK RHYME

A Cucumber's Pickle

Let us contemplate the sad fate
    Of the crisp, brisk, young cucumber,
Who lay in a leafy green field
    In blissful oblivious slumber
All of a sunshiny summer.

Who rudely was yanked from his bed,
    One of a very great number,
And thrown in a great bath of brine,
    (This happened in early September—
A terrible thing to remember!)

Slowly he felt himself change, it
    Made him increasingly glummer;
His temper got sour and mean—
    A pickle by early November!
A nosh for a butcher or plumber!

*

How like to ourselves, when Fate's finger, fickle,
Turns a young kook to a sour old pickle!

WILLIAM COLE

Who Ever Sausage a Thing?

One day a boy went walking
And went into a store;
He bought a pound of sausages
And laid them on the floor.

The boy began to whistle
A merry little tune—
And all the little sausages
Danced around the room!

ANONYMOUS

A Man for All Seasonings

"Pass the salt," I say, and yet
Salt and pepper's what I get.
If "Pass the pepper" I should yell,
Salt would come along as well.
Like man and wife, like sister, brother,
Where the one is, there's the other.
Though salt has many times the takers,
Pepper's in as many shakers.
So don't object, and don't be loath—
Just ask for one, accept them both.

RICHARD ARMOUR

36

Eat-It-All Elaine

I went away last August
To summer camp in Maine,
And there I met a camper
Called Eat-it-all Elaine.
Although Elaine was quiet,
She liked to cause a stir
By acting out the nickname
Her camp-mates gave to her.

The day of our arrival
At Cabin Number Three
When girls kept coming over
To greet Elaine and me,
She took a piece of Kleenex
And calmly chewed it up,
Then strolled outside the cabin
And ate a buttercup.

Elaine, from that day forward,
Was always in command.
On hikes, she'd eat some birch-bark
On swims, she'd eat some sand.
At meals, she'd swallow prune-pits
And never have a pain,
While everyone around her
Would giggle, "Oh, Elaine!"

One morning, berry-picking,
A bug was in her pail,
And though we thought for certain
Her appetite would fail,
Elaine said, "Hmm, a stinkbug."
And while we murmured, "Ooh,"
She ate her pail of berries
And ate the stinkbug, too.

The night of Final Banquet
When counselors were handing
Awards to different children
Whom they believed outstanding,
To every *thinking* person
At summer camp in Maine
The Most Outstanding Camper
Was Eat-it-all Elaine.

KAYE STARBIRD

The Teapot and the Kettle

Said the teapot to the kettle,
"You are really in fine fettle,
You're a handsome piece of metal
Are you not, not, not?

"Your dimensions are so spacious
And your waistline so capacious
And your whistle so flirtatious
When your water's hot."

Said the kettle, "Why you flatter
Me extremely, but no matter,
I have never seen a fatter
Teapot in my life.

"Though I would not call you dumpy,
You are round and sweet and plumpy
And I'm sure you're never grumpy.
Would you be my wife?"

Said the teapot to the kettle,
"Sir, my given name is Gretal
And I'd really like to settle
Down your wife to be."

So without the least delay
They were married the next day
And they both were very gay
Drinking tea, tea, tea.

MARY ANN HOBERMAN

JUST Married

If Walt Whitman
Had Written Humpty Dumpty

O Humpty! O Dumpty! You've had a fearful spill,
You've tumbled from the stony height,
    you're lying cold and still;
Your shell is cracked, your yolk runs out,
    your breath is faint and wheezy;
You landed as a scrambled egg, instead of over easy;
    The king has sent his steeds and men
        To mend you if they can;
           I pray that they did not forget
             To bring a frying pan.

FRANK JACOBS

It's such a shock, I almost screech,
When I find a worm inside my
    peach!
But then, what really makes me
    blue,
Is to find a worm who's bit in two!

WILLIAM COLE

I ate a ton of sugar.
It made me very sweet.
It also made me very round—
Now I cannot find my feet.

ALICE GILBERT

The Friendly Cinnamon Bun

Shining in his stickiness and glistening with honey,
Safe among his sisters and his brothers on a tray,
With raisin eyes that looked at me as I put down my
    money,
There smiled a friendly cinnamon bun, and this I
    heard him say:

"It's a lovely, lovely morning, and the world's a lovely
    place;
I know it's going to be a lovely day.
I know we're going to be good friends; I like your
    honest face;
Together we might go a long, long way."

The baker's girl rang up the sale. "I'll wrap your
    bun," said she.
"Oh no, you needn't bother," I replied.
I smiled back at that cinnamon bun and ate him, one
    two three,
And walked out with his friendliness inside.

RUSSELL HOBAN

Thoughts About Oysters

An oyster has no hands or feet
To put itself in motion.
It never waves or runs to meet
Companions in the ocean.

It has no mouth or nose or eyes
Like other water creatures,
Which makes it hard to recognize
An oyster by its features.

An oyster can't go any place.
It huddles in its shell;
And, though it hasn't got a face,
I guess it's just as well.

An oyster's personality
Is dull beyond expression;
And meeting oysters suddenly
You get a poor impression.

The gayest oyster never spends
Its time in fun or roistering,
Which means an oyster's only friends
Are people who go oystering.

The people greet it with a knife
And lemon juice—and therefore
I often think an oyster's life
Is not a life I'd care for.

KAYE STARBIRD

Recipe

I can make a sandwich.
I can really cook.
I made up this recipe
that should be in a book:
Take a jar of peanut butter.
Give it a spread,
until you have covered
a half a loaf of bread.

Pickles and pineapple,
strawberry jam,
salami and bologna
and half a pound of ham—
Pour some catsup on it.
Mix the mustard well.
Will it taste delicious?
Only you can tell.

BOBBI KATZ

Celery

Celery, raw,
Develops the jaw,
But celery, stewed,
Is more quietly chewed.

OGDEN NASH

Lemonade

Lemons all are yellow.
Lemons are afraid.
So squeeze a lemon gently
And give a lemonade.

PYKE JOHNSON, JR.

Menu
Roast Chicken
Ham
Pork Chops

Sold

SOLD

Point of View

Thanksgiving Dinner's sad and thankless
Christmas Dinner's dark and blue
When you stop and try to see it
From the turkey's point of view.

Sunday Dinner isn't sunny
Easter Feasts are just bad luck
When you see it from the viewpoint
Of a chicken or a duck.

Oh how I once loved tuna salad
Pork and lobsters—lamb chops too
Till I stopped and looked at dinner
From the dinner's point of view.

SHEL SILVERSTEIN

Lament, for Cocoa

The scum has come.
  My cocoa's cold.
The cup is numb,
  And I grow old.

It seems an age
  Since from the pot
It bubbled, beige
  And burning hot—

Too hot to be
  Too quickly quaffed.
Accordingly,
  I found a draft

And in it placed
  The boiling brew
And took a taste
  Of toast or two.

Alas, time flies
  And minutes chill;
My cocoa lies
  Dull brown and still.

How wearisome!
  In likelihood,
The scum, once come,
  Is come for good.

JOHN UPDIKE

Waiters

Dining with his older daughter
Dad forgot to order water.
Daughter quickly called the waiter.
Waiter said he'd bring it later.
So she waited, did the daughter,
Till the waiter brought her water.
When he poured it for her later,
Which one would you call the waiter?

MARY ANN HOBERMAN

Accidentally

Once—I didn't mean to,
but that
was that—
I yawned in the sunshine
and swallowed a gnat.

I'd rather eat mushrooms
and bullfrogs' legs,
I'd rather have pepper
all over my eggs

than open my mouth
on a sleepy day
and close on a gnat
going down that way.

It tasted sort of salty.
It didn't hurt a bit.
I accidentally ate a gnat.
and that
was
it!

MAXINE W. KUMIN

Table Manners

The Goops they lick their fingers,
 And the Goops they lick their knives;
They spill their broth on the table-cloth;
 Oh, they live untidy lives.
The Goops they talk while eating,
 And loud and fast they chew,
So that is why I am glad that I
 Am not a Goop. Are you?

GELETT BURGESS

Vegetables

Eat a tomato and you'll turn red
(I don't think that's really so);
Eat a carrot and you'll turn orange
(Still and all you never know);
Eat some spinach and you'll turn green
(I'm not saying that it's true
But that's what I heard, and so
I thought I'd pass it on to you).

SHEL SILVERSTEIN

An Alarming Sandwich

While munching my salami sub
I heard a small voice call, "Hey, bub,
Ahoy, ahoy! Are you the dope
Put mustard on my periscope?"

X. J. KENNEDY

Two Birds with One Stone

I don't like washing my ears,
But I do like quenching my thirst;
   I feel, when I've played,
   I could drink lemonade
In summer until I burst!

But a slice of watermelon
I think is especially swell!
   For it washes my ears
   Without soap or tears
And it quenches my thirst as well!

J. A. LINDON

Piggy

For breakfast I had ice cream
　　With pickles sliced up in it;
For lunch, some greasy pork chops
　　Gobbled in a minute;
Dinner? Clams and orange pop,
　　And liverwurst, sliced thick—
And now, oops! Oh, pardon me!
　　I'm going to be sick!

WILLIAM COLE

Anna Banana

Anna Banana, jump into the stew:
Gravy and carrots are *good* for you.
Good for your teeth, and your fingernails too,
So, Anna Banana, jump into the stew!

DENNIS LEE

The Groaning Board

A buttery, sugary, syrupy waffle—
Gee, but I love it somep'n awful.
Ginger-cakes dripping with chocolate goo,
Oo! How I love 'em! Oo! *Oo!* OO!

PINK

The Hot Pizza Serenade

(Sung to the tune of
"There's a Small Hotel")

There's a strange new dye
On my fav-rite tie—
I got it when I ate
Hot Pizza!

There's a glob of glue
On my new suede shoe—
I got it when I ate
Hot Pizza!

Each time that I eat it
   I am dropping Mozzarella!
I need an umbrella—
   Sloppy fella!

When my clothes have spots
Thick as polka dots,
I scrape the greasy stuff
From my collar, shirt and cuff,
And I know I've had enough
Hot Pizza!

FRANK JACOBS

Lasagna

Wouldn't you love
To have lasagna
Any old time
The mood was on ya?

X. J. KENNEDY

Some Cook!

Johnny made a custard
In the pepper pot.
Flavored it with mustard,
Put in quite a lot
Of garlic fried in olive oil,
Brought the custard to a boil,
Ate it up and burned his tongue—

You shouldn't cook when you're too young.

JOHN CIARDI

The Sausage

The sausage is a cunning bird
With feathers long and wavy;
It swims about the frying pan
And makes its nest in gravy.

ANONYMOUS

O Sliver of Liver

O sliver of liver,
Get lost! Go away!
You tremble and quiver
O sliver of liver—
You set me a-shiver
And spoil my day—
O sliver of liver,
Get lost! Go away!

MYRA COHN LIVINGSTON

Get Up, Get Up

Get up, get up, you lazy-head,
  Get up you lazy sinner,
We need those sheets for tablecloths,
  It's nearly time for dinner!

ANONYMOUS

Good Evening, Mr. Soup

(After "Good Morning, Mr. Zip, Zip, Zip")

Good evening, Mr. Soup, Soup, Soup,
  You taste about as good as ink;
Good evening, Mr. Soup, Soup, Soup,
  You're really awful weak, I think.
Yesterday they made you into Irish stew,
Today you come back to us, and taste like glue.
Good evening, Mr. Soup, Soup, Soup,
You taste about as good as—
You taste about as good as—
You taste about as good as ink.

BOY SCOUT SONG

Going Too *Far*

I could eat pails
of snails
cooked with garlic and butter—
they make my heart flutter—
with maybe a shallot
for my palate,
and parsley,
sparsely.

But I would never eat a slug!
Ugh!

WILLIAM COLE

Artichokes

I gave a dinner party
Where I served some arti-
chokes.
And the people burst out laughing,
Making rude remarks and
Jokes.

They cried, "These things could stick us."
Then they threw them on the
Floor.
And I became more angry
Than I'd ever been be-
fore.

I jumped up on the table
And I started in to
Shout,
Asking, "What were you expecting,
Hot dogs and sauer-
kraut?

"Sure, artichokes are prickly,
But I promise these won't
Hurt.
Now you pick them up and taste them
Or I won't give you des-
sert."

Then the people looked embarrassed
And they said they had to
Go,
Leaving artichokes all over
My new carpet down be-
low.

So I scooped them up and put them
On my bottom icebox shelf,
And now every day for breakfast
I enjoy one by my-
self.

PYKE JOHNSON, JR.

Through the Teeth

Through the teeth
And past the gums
Look out stomach,
Here it comes!

FOLK RHYME

Author Index

Title Index